Finding Love

How to Overcome Loneliness

Brigitte Novalis

Copyright 2009, 2011
by Brigitte Novalis

Acknowledgments

I thank Melissa Boynton for editing the English version of this book.

I thank Donna Casey for creating the cover.

Dear Reader,

Thank you for your interest in this book about finding love and overcoming loneliness. It is a short book but you find in it – like in a magical nutshell – everything you need to know about finding love.

Although it is easy and fun to read, you will also learn the vital principles which govern your relationships – with others and most importantly, with yourself.

Everything in your life is a result of what you know, what you experience, and how you act. Acting is not only what you do in physical terms, acting includes using your consciousness – your thoughts, emotions, and mental pictures.

Reading this book helps you to learn more about yourself and your relationships.

You will also understand *why* you experience loneliness in the first place and how to change it.

Most importantly, using the techniques in this book, you will bring friendship and love into your life.

This book is a transformative book. It is filled with positive energies. Your own energies become more positive as you read it.

Finding love is what you want – and you can have it!

Brigitte Novalis

"Live your dreams instead of merely dreaming about living."
- Bashar.

Table of Contents

Introduction

Chapter 1 - Who is lonely? Not me!

Chapter 2 - Becoming my own good friend – how would I do that?

Chapter 3 - Being my own good friend - what is the next step?

Chapter 4 - What about a little practice?

Chapter 5 - That spoils it all!

Chapter 6 - If I want to be more specific - what can I do?

Chapter 7 - The true source of love.

About the author

Who is lonely? Not me!

"Excuse me for asking, have we met before?"

"I don't think so, but you look familiar."

"I just checked the arrivals again. The plane is delayed for an hour. No wonder in this storm. Would you mind if we chat a bit while we wait?"

"That's fine".

"I'm waiting for a friend coming in from California. Who are you waiting for?"

"Ah, well, no one in particular."

"Is that so? How very interesting!"

"You think so? I come to the airport once in a while on the weekend, just to watch people".

"Are you a writer, observing people's behavior for a book?"

"No, I am just watching and listening, no particular reason."

"But you must get something out of it or you wouldn't drive all the way to the airport and spend time here."

"Sometimes I just enjoy being around people."

"So you don't have many people in your life?"

"I have colleagues at work."

"I hope you don't mind my saying that maybe you come here because you feel lonely at times?"

"No, I am not lonely. Definitely not. Well, sometimes, maybe. Just a little, when nobody is around. That's normal, isn't it - to feel a little lonely when you come home and there is no one there to greet you and everything is still dark unless you yourself turn on the lights? But can you really call that lonely? I mean it is not like I have no one in my life. I have family. Yes, I must admit, they don't live in my state but if I want to see them I can go and visit them for birthdays and holidays. And like everyone else, I have friends. Although I don't see them often, I

could see them if I want to. They would probably be happy to see me again after such a long time. Lonely? No, not me."

"Sorry for bringing it up. I just got the impression from these trips to the airport that you might feel a bit lonely and that you might want to do something about it, overcome it. That's all. I did not want to upset you. I apologize."

"No need to apologize. I think you meant well. In a way, you are right, you know. Truthfully, until you asked to chat I didn't realize that all the watching hasn't been enough. It is good to talk with someone who seems to care. You seem friendly and there aren't many friendly people out there. So, tell me about doing something about loneliness just as a matter of interest, of course. How would one overcome loneliness?"

"By stepping away from the loneliness. By stepping away, I don't mean going places or changing locations. I think of moving into another location within you, within your thinking and feeling."

"I can do that? How?"

"Easily. Everyone does it, but most of the time people are not aware they are doing it."

"Hmm... sounds interesting. So, how do I do that?"

"Let me give you an example. Let's say it's a rainy day and you long for sunshine. Even though it is raining outside, you can close your eyes for a moment and imagine sunshine: you can see in your mind the blue sky. You can feel the warmth of the sun on your skin, if you wish. You can also feel the inner joy of bathing in the sunshine. You can do this, and more, in your mind."

"Oh, you are talking about imagination! I thought you were talking about something real!"

"Imagination IS real. Everything that you see around you, the chair you sit in, the walls of your house, have first been in the imagination of someone before the walls were raised to build the house or before the wood was put together to make the chair. First the thought, then the picture in the mind, and then the physical object."

"Interesting thought. But coming back to loneliness, are you suggesting that if I want friendship or love, I could just imagine having someone in my life, and that's all?"

"That's a good start."
"But I don't want to have imaginary friends; I want to have real friends."

"If you want to have friends, keep this in mind:

In order to have good friends,
you have to become
your own good friend."

Chapter 2

Becoming my own good friend – how would I do that?

"Becoming my own good friend – how would I do that? Is there something to do or to learn?"

"Indeed. Let's have a look at your relationships with friends right now. You mentioned your friends and that you have not seem them in a while. Why is that?"

"I don't know. I think I just lost interest."

"Can you think back to the last time when you were with your friends? Yes? Good. When you think of this time together, how do you feel?"

"To tell you the truth, the movie was kind of nice and the food was not too bad, and I suppose the company was ok but I don't feel anything in particular. It wasn't great or pleasant. That is why I haven't seen them in a while. Being with them left me feeling a little empty."

"Do you know why?"

"I have no idea."

"Can it be that you were already feeling empty inside?"

"I don't understand."

"Let me ask you a different question: did you feel good meeting your friends? Did you feel really good and happy?"

"Well, I expected them to be fun but they weren't."

"What about YOU being fun?"

"I didn't feel so good then."

"And now?"

"I don't feel so good now."

"Would you like to feel better?"

"Of course! What a question!"

"Are you willing to try something right away? Good. Let's start with something easy. I would like you to go to the nearest mirror and smile at yourself."

"You want me to go smile at myself in the mirror? I can't do that. What if someone saw me?"

"Well, you can wash your hands for a while until you are alone and then smile at yourself. That does not take much time to do."

"That's it? Just smile at myself? And what good would that do?"

"Why don't you find out yourself?"

"Okay, since I have nothing better to do at the moment, I'll humor you."

*****

"So, you are back. How was it?"

"Embarrassing somehow. Even though I was by myself I felt embarrassed, smiling at myself. It was weird. On the other hand, it didn't feel so bad either. Interesting..."

"Well done! Are you ready for the next step?"

"What would that be?"

"Go back to the mirror, smile at yourself and say "I love you" out loud."

"Wait a minute! You want me to make a fool of myself? To say out loud in public that I love myself?"

"Well, you can wait until you are alone. Don't be so concerned about others. You have your own life to live, not theirs, right?"

"Wow, this just gets weirder and weirder. Don't look at me so disapprovingly. Okay, I'll do it."

*****

"It took you a while to come back. What happened?"

"It took me a while because people came in and people went out and then I was all by myself and I still couldn't say it. It took several attempts to say it. It felt so embarrassing, so wrong to say something like that to myself. So phony..."

"But I did not want to be a coward; I knew you were waiting for me to come back. So I said it finally. And then I cried. When I said, "I love you" to myself, I cried. Have you ever heard anything so stupid?"

"I don't find it stupid to cry. What I find really stupid is NOT to love yourself."

"You have a point there; but may I come back to loneliness? What does saying "I love you" to myself have to do with escaping loneliness?"

"The answer is simple:

>   ***If you don't love yourself –***
>   ***how can you like or love others?"***

"Oh, I see. You are telling me that loneliness has something to do with me? It's not circumstances or other people's weird behavior – it's mine?"

"Yes, that is what I think. Let me ask you:

>   ***If you don't love yourself –***
>   ***how can you expect***
>   ***others to love you?"***

"I never thought about such things before but it makes sense to me. Sad to say, it seems I don't love myself very much. When I stepped in front of the mirror and said: "I love you" at your request, it felt phony. It was disturbing for me to notice that I had such a hard time saying it – let alone feeling it! So this self-love is really missing in my life. Funny that I did not notice it earlier. So, I am a lost case, right?"

"Not at all! You can always make changes."

"I can? But what can I do?"

"You can start being your own good friend. Smile at yourself and tell yourself every day, several times a day that you love yourself."

"That would make a difference?"

"What do you think?"

"Well, it might.   I feel a bit better already. It is worth a try. Nothing to lose, right?"

Chapter 3

Being my own good friend – what is the next step?

"Look. Here come some more people. I don't want you to miss your friend. Let's take a quick look at the board with the arrivals."

"Oh good, the plane has not yet landed. So, we still have some time to talk if that's okay with you."

"Certainly. My pleasure."

"Now, suppose I do this smiling into the mirror and saying "I love you" to myself – what is the next step? There must be more to it than that, right?"

"You are right. There are more steps. One of these steps is that you start enjoying your life."

"Enjoying my life – could you be more concrete?"

"Let's start with something simple. What did you like to do when you were a little child?"

"Well – may I ask you what that has to do with overcoming loneliness?"

"Many things. Your feelings of loneliness may be the same feelings you had as a small child. Can you remember being seven years old?"

"Yes, I can. Back then, I didn't feel lonely. Unhappy perhaps."

"You are able to remember the little child you were because this little child still lives in your deeper mind. You might not think of her everyday but if you make a conscious effort to remember her, you can do so. This little child you were is a part of you now. If she was unhappy in the past, you can make her happy now."

"How?"

"What did she like to do most of all?"

"Let me think. Ah, I know! I liked to sit by the stream behind my grand-parents' house. I liked that a lot. I could stay there all by myself for hours on end, gazing at the water as it swirled around the rocks. I also liked to

listen to the sound of the water. What a wonderful sound that was!"

"Have you been there lately?"

"No, my grandparents passed away a long time ago. I have not been to any stream for a very long time."

"Why not? You still like sitting by a stream, right?"

"Yes, I would like it but I have other things to do. I have my job. Then I have errands to run, and take care of my house. There are only so many hours in the day, you know."

"What about weekends – you don't work on the weekends, do you?"

"Well, on weekends - yes, I could have driven back to that place. But why bother? Driving for more than an hour just for myself?"

"Why do you say "why bother?" Are you not important enough to yourself?"

"If you put it that way — I should be important to myself, right? Why am I not? Why didn't I consider driving to that stream at least once? I don't know. Is it laziness?"

"Imagine, please, for a moment that you have a very dear friend and this friend tells you: "I would love to sit by a stream. That would be so lovely but without you I cannot get there." What would you do?"

"I would drive my friend to the stream at the first opportunity. Yes, I want to be kind to myself. I really do. I don't know why I never thought of this. In the past, I thought that it

was silly and selfish to do something out of the ordinary for myself. As if I didn't deserve it. But you are right; I have to be my own good friend in order to be a good friend to others, right? I still have a question, though. How does it work? Suppose I am kind to myself and start loving myself, how would that help me find the right friends?"

"It works because of the Law of Attraction. Have you heard about it?"

"Yes, someone at work mentioned it. They talked about a movie called "The Secret". They were all so excited about it. But to tell the truth, I don't know how this works. It sounds a little silly to me that I think about something and imagine a situation and then it happens to me. Impossible!"

"Why do you think it is impossible?"

"It's obvious, isn't it? What I think happens in my head, right? And when I imagine something that also happens in my head. Thoughts are - what can I say? – flimsy things. They are without substance. Or better, without any force behind them. How can my thoughts make something happen?"

"Your thoughts don't just happen in your head. They radiate out of you. You are like a walking TV tower, radiating out what you think and feel."

"Are you saying that people know what I think and feel?"

"To a certain degree, yes. The more sensitive people are, they more they are able to pick up your thoughts and emotions."

"Amazing! Is that the Law of Attraction?"

"There is more to it. The Law of Attraction says "like attracts like". In a nutshell – you feel good and good things come your way."

"The opposite is also true. The more people worry, the more things and situations they attract to worry about."

"I am beginning to understand what you're saying. So when I am kind to myself and love myself – this shines out of me. Then I attract friends? I lost you there."

**"The more "kindness and love energy"
you shine out,
the more of this good energy
comes back to you."**

"Interesting. So, if I want friends and maybe even a best friend, all I have to do is to say to myself: "I love, I love you", and then they show up in my life?"

"If you do this only on a surface level – not really feeling the good feeling that goes along with saying and thinking "I love you", then nothing is achieved. Energy is real and emotional energy is also real. It is positive or negative. Either it feels good or it feels bad. You cannot pretend it. The good news is that when you really intend to feel good about yourself – or other people or situations – and you repeat positive thoughts, then you start feeling good."

"Why is that?"

"Because energy follows thought."

"That is so interesting! I hope I learn this soon."

"If you really want to make a lasting change in your life, you will learn it."

"I want to have good friends. I really do."

Chapter 4

What about a little practice?

"Would you like to start practicing what you have learned right now?"

"I would love to – but right here?"

"Why not? If you close your eyes for a moment, people won't notice.   Just say to yourself with as much love as you can muster: "I love you, I love you". After a while, you will feel good. Then let me know, please."

*****

"I feel good. That's interesting, I really feel good!"

"Well done! You may open your eyes. What I want you to do now is look around at people with kindness as if you think that they are all great people. Don't make it too obvious, though. Just look around casually and think: "You are great people". Remember to feel what you are thinking."

"Okay. I will give it a try."

"Well, how are you doing?"

"It's difficult. I did not notice earlier how difficult it is to like people. With some I have no problems, but with others! They look so self-important or angry or mean. How can I like them?"

"Do you think that judging people is good for you or for them?"

"I'm not judging them. I'm just looking at them. You can't help noticing how they are, right?"

"People have many facets. They are angry at one time, they are friendly at another time. Would you like me to tell you how I saw you when I first looked at you?"

"You mean what I looked like?"

"Yes, in a way, but more than that. The impression I got from you."

"Well, how was it?"

"You looked sad, withdrawn, and even a little hostile."

"I did?"

"Then I took a closer look and I saw that you were just lonely."

"And you still wanted to talk with me?"

"Yes, I did."

"But why?"

"When I looked at you with, how should I say it, the eyes of my heart or my intuition, I noticed how wonderful you are."

"I am?"

"Yes, you are. I want you now to look at these people with those same kind eyes."

"How exactly would I do this?"

"When you love and appreciate yourself enough, it is easy for you to love and appreciate others as well. I don't expect you to love all the people who are coming through the gates or who are waiting for friends or family to arrive. But you could feel a certain kindness towards them."

"I think I know what you mean. I can come into this "mood of kindness" when I love myself, right? Okay, let me try."

*****

"This is interesting. People seem to be somehow nicer and prettier now. But it's not them, it's me, right?"

"It's both."

"It's both? Now you've confused me. How can it be both?"

"When you look at them with kind eyes or with appreciation, you see the good in them. People are good. They are just a bit lonely or frightened at times.

"Also, when you look at them with kind eyes, people are somehow aware of this kindness directed towards them. They respond to this kindness - like flowers turning their faces towards the sun.   You can perceive this intuitively."

"Well – I don't know. Are you saying that everyone will respond to kindness?"

"Perhaps not everyone. You see, people have choices. Most people, however, want to be appreciated, want to feel good."

"Let me make sure I've got this straight. When I love myself and others, then others will love or at least like me, too?"

"You said it very well. But do not to try to manipulate people. You have to be sincere and let them be the way they want to be."

"You want me to let them be the way they want to be? You are kidding, right?"

Chapter 5

That spoils it all!

"I'm afraid that spoils it all."

"What on earth do you mean?"

"You just said that I have to let them – the people in my life - be the way they want to be.

"What's wrong with that?"

"I want them to be good to me – kind, understanding, generous, and pleasant. I don't want to let them be the way they are!"

"And how do YOU want to be?"

"I also want to be good to them in return – naturally!"

"That's good! If you are all of this: good and pleasant and generous and understanding, then – by the Law of Attraction – that is how the people in your life will be."

"So they will behave as I want them to behave?"

"Excuse me, please. Are you looking for friends or for slaves?"

"Good point. But what do you think I CAN expect from future friends?"

"In some ways your friends will be similar to you. Do you know the saying: "Birds of a feather flock together"?"

"I do."

"Also know that, in some ways your friends - or your partner or your children, for that matter - will be different from you. And that is good, isn't it? Where would the excitement, the thrill, and the inspiration of a relationship be if your friends did not bring new thoughts, tastes and ideas into your life? And your influence into their lives?"

"When you put it that way, yes – but I don't want mean people in my life! I know we just mentioned the saying "Birds of a feather flock together", so when I am good I can expect good people to come into my life. But I have to tell you that years ago I had a boyfriend *who really didn't treat me well. What do you say to that?"*

"Before this man came into your life – did you feel good about yourself? Were you loving yourself? Being kind to yourself?"

"No, I had a bad time that year. I felt sad and lonely. I thought that if..."

"Well?"

"I thought that if I had a boyfriend, I would feel better. But it didn't work out that way and I am starting to understand why. If I feel bad, I cannot attract someone good into my life, right? That's so because of the Law of Attraction. Like attracts like."

"That's right."

"Now I feel really terrible. Does that mean that I was bad at that time?"

"No, you are good. What you did was send out negative vibes, feelings of sadness and loneliness. Do you remember how to start sending out positive vibes?"

"By loving myself?"

"Yes, by loving yourself."

"Loving myself will do the job? It's that powerful?"

"Loving and appreciating yourself and others – that is the most powerful energy there is. And you can do it!"

"You are right. I can do it."

Chapter 6

If I want to be more specific, what can I do?

"I think I understand it now. When I feel good and loving and happy then I send out good and loving and happy vibes, right?"

"Right. You got it!"

"And then these good vibes come back to me. By the way, how exactly?"

"In the form of good people, events and circumstances."

"Does that mean that I get a whole new set of friends?"

"Not necessarily. Mostly, the people who are already in your life will just start showing you their best side."

"You mean they will be nicer to me than before? How can they suddenly be nicer? Do I change them somehow?"

"They respond to the new and better vibrations you send out."

"Honestly, I don't really understand this. How is it possible? Can you explain how it works?"

"Imagine that each human being is like a large living crystal. The more light is in the crystal, the brighter the crystal shines. Also, the crystal has many facets. Some are dark and murky, others shine in clear bright colors. As you love yourself and others more and more this can be compared to the crystal getting brighter and brighter."

"Wait a minute! The crystals don't shine by themselves, right? They reflect light. I thought crystals only get brighter when light shines on them."

"Did you notice that some crystals are clearer and brighter than others? When light shines on them, they reflect more light, that means they shine brighter."

"Oh, now I know what you are driving at. As I love myself and others more, the crystal that I am, so to speak, gets brighter."

"Yes, and when this happens other human crystals respond to your brightness and turn around a bit and show you their own bright facets."

"Cool. That happens every time?"

"Most of the time but not every time. Remember that people have free will. Some may decide not to show you their brighter facets which means, they don't want to like you more."

"And some may not even have brighter facets!"

"True."

"What happens then? Do I have to put up with grumpy people?"

"If you continue loving yourself and others, these grumpy people will usually drift out of your life. You might see them less often or they might become less important for you. Some might even move to another town."

"*Does that mean I will have less people in my life?*"

"No, when some drift away, others will come to take their place."

"*That's fascinating, isn't it? To think that I have such influence over others.*"

"Do you know, the words "influence over others" sound a bit like manipulation again. Remember, this is more about being at your best and bringing out the best in others."

"*I agree. That's what I want. Now, if I want to be more specific, what can I do?*"

"More specific meaning …?"

"Attracting a partner. Someone I can happily share my life with. Do you have a suggestion for that?"

"A good suggestion. You could even call it a master plan."

"I like the sound of that! Please tell me. What can I do?"

"You can use your imagination. In order to reach your goal, you have to be persistent, though."

"I can be persistent. If that brings my partner to me, I definitely will be persistent. What steps do I need to take?"

"Every day, in the morning and again at night, I want you to focus on the partnership you want. Picture this special person with you. Imagine yourself with your partner walking along the

beach or in a park, even just strolling through your neighborhood."

"That's easy! I can do that! What else?"

"You can picture yourself with your partner shopping or cooking or dancing."

"Sorry. I'm not good at dancing."

"You are free to choose what you want to imagine. By the way, when you imagine yourself dancing well, you will dance better eventually."

"So, I imagine myself being with my partner every day, in the morning and in the evening. Is that all?"

"That is the first step. The next step is *feeling* **it."**

"What do you mean by feeling it?"

"Keep your picture in your mind until you *feel* **the happy and comfortable feeling of having your partner by your side."**

"How can I feel good about something that is not there? At least not there yet?"

"Your partner is with you in your mind, right?"

"Well, yes."

"Your mind is powerful enough to create both the image and the feeling. This feeling good about what you are imagining takes a little practice but you wanted to take the next step, right?"

"Yes, right! Please go on. How do I do this feeling thing?"

"As you imagine vividly being with your partner, you start feeling good as if your partner were already there. Go to that good feeling more often during the day. Remember, in your mind you can go to new places if you wish."

"I do remember that we talked about that. I can do it. And then what happens?"

"As you feel this good feeling of companionship more often, your partner will show up eventually."

"Wow! Great! That's all?"

"You also have to take action. Go places so you can create opportunities to meet your partner. They will not knock at your door as you sit on your sofa watching TV."

"Thank you so much for sharing this with me! I already feel much better. Now I know what

to do. That should be easy. I imagine my partner every day and get into this good feeling. Soon, there will be no more loneliness for me!"

"Haven't you forgotten something?"

"What do you mean?"

"The precondition for any good and enjoyable relationship is love. You have to practice loving yourself and others."

"*Right! I understand. I have to learn to shine on my own before I can attract another person who is also shining from within; the type of person who will be a loving, caring partner for me."*

"Well said. I'm glad that you understand this."

"Oh, there are so many people coming through the gate. Maybe they are from the flight you're waiting for."

"Yes, there's my friend coming. It was a pleasure talking with you. Good luck!"

"Excuse me, I'd really like to talk again sometime. If you are planning to bring your friend back to the airport, do you mind if I meet you here?"

"Good idea! Yes, let's talk some more. The flight back is in ten days, around 10 am. Could you meet me back here at that time?"

"I will make it happen, believe me. This is important, worth taking a few hours off work. Before we part – what would you suggest is the most important thing for me to do in the meantime?"

"Love and appreciate yourself and everyone and everything around you and imagine your partner being in your life already. Just give it a try. It's fun!"

"Will do. See you soon!"

Chapter 7

The true source of love

"I'm so glad that we can sit here comfortably over coffee and talk. For a while I was afraid I would not see you again. But then there you were - seeing your friend off."

"I'm also glad we met. How have you been doing? Have you practiced the loving and appreciating?"

"I did! Over and over again! I wanted to find out if it really works."

"During the past ten days I said in my mind over and over "I love you, I love you" to myself, coworkers and friends and even to frustrating situations; of course, not all the time, but very often. I think that helped me to really appreciate myself and others. You can be proud of me."

"I am. So, how are you doing?"

"I feel better than I have for a long time. I even sleep better. Many things are changing. People at work are nicer, even my boss seems to have more patience. I suppose, I am nicer, too. Thank you for pointing these things out to me. I never imagined I could do something to make myself feel better. I always felt like it was other people's actions or even just luck. I feel good from the inside out."

"I'm so glad to hear that."

"I have a question, though. I've always wanted to be loved by others. What you taught me to do was love myself, right? Now, what about being loved by others?"

"When you say you want to be loved by others – what is it that you want to FEEL?"

"I want to feel their love, of course"

"Please imagine for a moment that there is a person in your life whom you don't care for very much, if at all. When this person sends you flowers, presents, letters, emails saying "I love you" – what do you feel?"

"Give me a moment. What would I feel? At first I might be flattered but over time it would be a nuisance!"

"You wouldn't feel love?"

"No. I think I know what you are driving at. To feel love, I have to love, right? So, the true source of love is loving myself?"

"And then loving others while you gracefully receive their love."

"In the past, I got it all wrong. No wonder I felt so lonely! Thank you so much for helping me understand more about love!"

"You are most welcome. May I ask you about loneliness? Do you still feel lonely?"

"In a way I don't feel lonely, maybe once in a while. Then I remember our conversation and I start doing the loving and appreciating. That makes me feel good again. I am also following your "master plan". Every morning and every evening I imagine having my partner by my side. Last week something

happened I'd like to share with you. Do you have a bit more time?"

"Absolutely. I can't wait to hear it!"

"Well, there is this young man in my neighborhood. He walks his puppy on my street. Sometimes, when I come home, he walks by and his dog jumps at me – she is on the leash, but still – I don't like that. So, one day I told him: "I don't like your dog jumping on me." And he said: "She is only a puppy. She just wants to play." So, I said: "Well, I don't like dogs." He made an annoyed face and walked on. Since then, he walks on the other side of the street and does not look at me."

"In the meantime, I continued loving myself and everyone else and imagining my partner by my side.

"And, then, guess what happened? One evening, as I was practicing my loving and appreciating on my walk home from the train, he and his puppy came along and I couldn't help smiling at them. I don't know why I stopped and talked to him but I did. I said: "You are right. She is pretty cute and just being curious." So he got very friendly and we talked a bit.

"The next evening, here they are again, and we talk some more. I even walked with them one night and he invited me for a cup of coffee tonight. Isn't that great?"

"I'm so happy for you. Well done!"

"Thank you. Do you know what the best part is?"

"Please tell me."

"The best part is the change in me. Of course, I'm looking forward to seeing him tonight and talking over coffee. To tell the truth, I am a little nervous about it. But before, I would fret and worry constantly about "what if?" Usually, when I went for a first date, I had terrible scenarios in my mind of all kinds of discomfort and misunderstandings.

"Now I am just happy to see him and his puppy again. Well, with some nervousness mixed in. But that is natural, right? Does he become a friend or even a boyfriend? Maybe. I would like that because he seems to be kind and caring. He is also cute like his puppy.

"But the best part is that I feel good regardless – whether or not we become friends. You know what I mean?"

"I know exactly what you mean. I'm so happy for you."

"And I am so grateful to you! You showed me how to find love and overcome loneliness and it works! I know, I have to continue doing it – this loving and appreciating and imagining, but it's worth it!"

"I'm glad that you understand this now."

"Meeting you has been life changing. Thank you for sharing your thoughts with me. Sometimes I think we were meant to meet."

"Yes, I think so, too."

"Hey, wait a minute, "meant to meet"? Is this the Law of Attraction? Did I attract you?"

"By all means! When you are ready for positive changes, you attract people – or books – that can help you to change."

"So I find love and overcome loneliness because I am ready for change?"

"Being ready for changes
opens the door.
Understanding
how life works
puts you on your path.
Practicing and living
what you have learned
brings about the change."

"So the real change has happened because I started loving myself and others?"

"Yes, exactly."

"Thank you so much for helping me along! I feel so good now – freer, more peaceful and

more lovable. Do you know, for the first time in many years I feel that life is good."

About the Author

Brigitte Novalis has spent her life being a catalyst of change. Since childhood she has been aware of her ability to bring peace and harmony into her environment.

Her love of nature and concern for the planet led her to a career in environmental politics. Her work helped to create a new and more positive way to look at our environment and resulted in the building of the first German recycling plant, setting into motion a shift in environmental awareness that began in Germany and spread throughout all of Europe.

Realizing that the problem of pollution is a mere symptom of the larger struggles in humanity, Novalis turned her focus towards personal and spiritual development. She explored and studied the body-mind-soul connection with the conviction that large-scale shifts in humankind can only come from within.

In her books, Brigitte Novalis shares her two gifts: the gift of healing and the gift of writing. The synergy* that comes from the two combined gifts has a healing and transformative effect on the reader.

Brigitte Novalis is not only a published author and an intuitive healer; she is also an accomplished therapist: Neurolinguistic Psychology, Clinical Hypnotherapy, and Reiki Master Level.

She is the founder of the Alpha Center for Personal Development in Quincy, MA. Most importantly, she has created her own healing system, the Multi Level Transformation system.

synergism: the interaction of elements that when combined produce a total effect that is greater than the sum of the individual elements, contributions, etc.

Connect with Brigitte online:

Website and blog:
http://www.brigittenovalis.com/